This Wedding Planner Belongs To:

♥ _____ ♥

_____

Initial Planning Phase

IDEAS FOR THEME

IDEAS FOR VENUE

IDEAS FOR COLORS

IDEAS FOR MUSIC

IDEAS FOR RECEPTION

OTHER IDEAS

Notes & Ideas

Wedding Budget Planner

Expense MANAGER

CATEGORY/ITEMS	BUDGET	ACTUAL COST	BALANCE

Wedding Budget Checklist

CATEGORY	BUDGET	ACTUAL COST	DEPOSIT	BALANCE

Wedding Contact List

IMPORTANT VENDOR CONTACTS				
	NAME	PHONE #	EMAIL	ADDRESS
OFFICIANT				
RECEPTION VENUE				
WEDDING SHOP				
TAILOR				
FLORIST				
CATERER				
DJ/ENTERTAINMENT				
WEDDING VENUE				
TRANSPORTATION				
OTHER:				
OTHER:				
OTHER:				

NOTES & More

SPECIAL REMINDERS

Planning Snapshot

CEREMONY EXPENSE TRACKER

	BUDGET	COST	DEPOSIT	BALANCE	DUE DATE
OFFICIANT GRATUITY					
MARRIAGE LICENSE					
VENUE COST					
FLOWERS					
DECORATIONS					
OTHER					

NOTES & Reminders

NOTES & REMINDERS

RECEPTION EXPENSE TRACKER

	BUDGET	COST	DEPOSIT	BALANCE	DUE DATE
VENUE FEE					
CATERING/FOOD					
BAR/BEVERAGES					
CAKE/CUTTING FEE					
DECORATIONS					
RENTALS/EXTRAS					
BARTENDER/STAFF					

NOTES & More

SPECIAL REMINDERS

Planning Snapshot

PAPER PRODUCTS EXPENSE TRACKER

	BUDGET	COST	DEPOSIT	BALANCE	DUE DATE
INVITATIONS/CARDS					
POSTAGE COSTS					
THANK YOU CARDS					
PLACE CARDS					
GUESTBOOK					
OTHER					

NOTES & Reminders

NOTES & REMINDERS

ENTERTAINMENT EXPENSE TRACKER

	BUDGET	COST	DEPOSIT	BALANCE	DUE DATE
BAND/DJ					
SOUND SYSTEM RENTAL					
VENUE/DANCE RENTAL					
GRATUITIES					
OTHER:					
OTHER:					
OTHER:					

NOTES & More

SPECIAL REMINDERS

Planning Snapshot

WEDDING PARTY ATTIRE EXPENSE TRACKER

	BUDGET	COST	DEPOSIT	BALANCE	DUE DATE
TUX RENTALS					
BRIDESMAN SUIT					
SHOES					
VEIL/GARTER/OTHER					
ALTERATION COSTS					

NOTES & Reminders

NOTES & REMINDERS

TRANSPORTATION EXPENSE TRACKER

	BUDGET	COST	DEPOSIT	BALANCE	DUE DATE
LIMO RENTAL					
VALET PARKING					
VENUE TRANSPORTATION					
AIRPORT TRANSPORTATION					
OTHER:					
OTHER:					
OTHER:					

NOTES & More

SPECIAL REMINDERS

Planning Snapshot

FLORIST EXPENSE TRACKER					
	BUDGET	COST	DEPOSIT	BALANCE	DUE DATE
VENUE DECORATIONS					
BOUTONNIERES					
VASES/EXTRAS					
TABLE DECORATIONS					
OTHER:					

NOTES & Reminders

NOTES & REMINDERS

OTHER EXPENSE TRACKER					
	BUDGET	COST	DEPOSIT	BALANCE	DUE DATE
PHOTOGRAPHER					
VIDEOGRAPHER					
CATERER					
HAIR/SALON					
WEDDING RINGS					
WEDDING PARTY GIFTS					
OTHER:					

NOTES & More

SPECIAL REMINDERS

Groom's Planner

HAIR APPOINTMENT

SALON NAME	DATE	TIME	BOOKED FOR:	ADDRESS:
			☐	
			☐	
			☐	

NOTES

TUX FITTING APPOINTMENT

BUSINESS NAME	DATE	TIME	BOOKED FOR:	ADDRESS:
			☐	
			☐	

NOTES

OTHER:

BUSINESS NAME	DATE	TIME	BOOKED FOR:	ADDRESS:
			☐	
			☐	
			☐	

NOTES

Important Dates

DATE:	DATE:	DATE:	REMINDERS
DATE:	DATE:	DATE:	
DATE:	DATE:	DATE:	
			NOTES
DATE:	DATE:	DATE:	
DATE:	DATE:	DATE:	

Weekly Wedding Planning

WEEK OF: ....

MONDAY

WEDDING TO DO LIST

- [ ] ....
- [ ] ....
- [ ] ....
- [ ] ....
- [ ] ....
- [ ] ....
- [ ] ....
- [ ] ....
- [ ] ....
- [ ] ....
- [ ] ....
- [ ] ....
- [ ] ....
- [ ] ....
- [ ] ....
- [ ] ....

TUESDAY

WEDNESDAY

THURSDAY

APPOINTMENTS & MEETINGS

DATE	TIME	VENDOR	PURPOSE

FRIDAY

SATURDAY

Weekly Wedding Planning

WEEK OF: _____

MONDAY

TUESDAY

WEDNESDAY

THURSDAY

FRIDAY

SATURDAY

WEDDING TO DO LIST

- ☐ _____
- ☐ _____
- ☐ _____
- ☐ _____
- ☐ _____
- ☐ _____
- ☐ _____
- ☐ _____
- ☐ _____
- ☐ _____
- ☐ _____
- ☐ _____
- ☐ _____
- ☐ _____
- ☐ _____

APPOINTMENTS & MEETINGS			
DATE	TIME	VENDOR	PURPOSE

Weekly Wedding Planning

WEEK OF: ....

MONDAY

WEDDING TO DO LIST

- [ ] _____
- [ ] _____
- [ ] _____
- [ ] _____
- [ ] _____
- [ ] _____
- [ ] _____
- [ ] _____
- [ ] _____
- [ ] _____
- [ ] _____
- [ ] _____
- [ ] _____
- [ ] _____
- [ ] _____
- [ ] _____

TUESDAY

WEDNESDAY

APPOINTMENTS & MEETINGS

DATE	TIME	VENDOR	PURPOSE

THURSDAY

FRIDAY

SATURDAY

Weekly Wedding Planning

WEEK OF: ....

MONDAY

TUESDAY

WEDNESDAY

THURSDAY

FRIDAY

SATURDAY

WEDDING TO DO LIST

- ☐ _____
- ☐ _____
- ☐ _____
- ☐ _____
- ☐ _____
- ☐ _____
- ☐ _____
- ☐ _____
- ☐ _____
- ☐ _____
- ☐ _____
- ☐ _____
- ☐ _____
- ☐ _____
- ☐ _____

APPOINTMENTS & MEETINGS

DATE	TIME	VENDOR	PURPOSE

Weekly Wedding Planning

WEEK OF: ....

MONDAY

TUESDAY

WEDNESDAY

THURSDAY

FRIDAY

SATURDAY

WEDDING TO DO LIST

- [ ] _____
- [ ] _____
- [ ] _____
- [ ] _____
- [ ] _____
- [ ] _____
- [ ] _____
- [ ] _____
- [ ] _____
- [ ] _____
- [ ] _____
- [ ] _____
- [ ] _____
- [ ] _____
- [ ] _____

APPOINTMENTS & MEETINGS

DATE	TIME	VENDOR	PURPOSE

Weekly Wedding Planning

WEEK OF: _____

MONDAY

TUESDAY

WEDNESDAY

THURSDAY

FRIDAY

SATURDAY

WEDDING TO DO LIST

- ☐ _____
- ☐ _____
- ☐ _____
- ☐ _____
- ☐ _____
- ☐ _____
- ☐ _____
- ☐ _____
- ☐ _____
- ☐ _____
- ☐ _____
- ☐ _____
- ☐ _____
- ☐ _____
- ☐ _____

APPOINTMENTS & MEETINGS

DATE	TIME	VENDOR	PURPOSE

Weekly Wedding Planning

WEEK OF: ....

MONDAY

TUESDAY

WEDNESDAY

THURSDAY

FRIDAY

SATURDAY

WEDDING TO DO LIST

- ☐ ....
- ☐ ....
- ☐ ....
- ☐ ....
- ☐ ....
- ☐ ....
- ☐ ....
- ☐ ....
- ☐ ....
- ☐ ....
- ☐ ....
- ☐ ....
- ☐ ....
- ☐ ....
- ☐ ....

APPOINTMENTS & MEETINGS

DATE	TIME	VENDOR	PURPOSE

Weekly Wedding Planning

WEEK OF: _____

MONDAY

TUESDAY

WEDNESDAY

THURSDAY

FRIDAY

SATURDAY

WEDDING TO DO LIST

- ☐ _____
- ☐ _____
- ☐ _____
- ☐ _____
- ☐ _____
- ☐ _____
- ☐ _____
- ☐ _____
- ☐ _____
- ☐ _____
- ☐ _____
- ☐ _____
- ☐ _____
- ☐ _____
- ☐ _____
- ☐ _____

APPOINTMENTS & MEETINGS

DATE	TIME	VENDOR	PURPOSE

Weekly Wedding Planning

WEEK OF: ....

MONDAY

TUESDAY

WEDNESDAY

THURSDAY

FRIDAY

SATURDAY

WEDDING TO DO LIST

- [ ] _____
- [ ] _____
- [ ] _____
- [ ] _____
- [ ] _____
- [ ] _____
- [ ] _____
- [ ] _____
- [ ] _____
- [ ] _____
- [ ] _____
- [ ] _____
- [ ] _____
- [ ] _____
- [ ] _____

APPOINTMENTS & MEETINGS

DATE	TIME	VENDOR	PURPOSE

Weekly Wedding Planning

WEEK OF: ....

MONDAY

TUESDAY

WEDNESDAY

THURSDAY

FRIDAY

SATURDAY

WEDDING TO DO LIST

- ☐
- ☐
- ☐
- ☐
- ☐
- ☐
- ☐
- ☐
- ☐
- ☐
- ☐
- ☐
- ☐
- ☐
- ☐
- ☐

APPOINTMENTS & MEETINGS			
DATE	TIME	VENDOR	PURPOSE

Weekly Wedding Planning

WEEK OF: _____

MONDAY

TUESDAY

WEDNESDAY

THURSDAY

FRIDAY

SATURDAY

WEDDING TO DO LIST

- [ ] _____
- [ ] _____
- [ ] _____
- [ ] _____
- [ ] _____
- [ ] _____
- [ ] _____
- [ ] _____
- [ ] _____
- [ ] _____
- [ ] _____
- [ ] _____
- [ ] _____
- [ ] _____
- [ ] _____
- [ ] _____

APPOINTMENTS & MEETINGS

DATE	TIME	VENDOR	PURPOSE

Weekly Wedding Planning

WEEK OF: _____

MONDAY

TUESDAY

WEDNESDAY

THURSDAY

FRIDAY

SATURDAY

WEDDING TO DO LIST

- [ ] _____
- [ ] _____
- [ ] _____
- [ ] _____
- [ ] _____
- [ ] _____
- [ ] _____
- [ ] _____
- [ ] _____
- [ ] _____
- [ ] _____
- [ ] _____
- [ ] _____
- [ ] _____
- [ ] _____

APPOINTMENTS & MEETINGS

DATE	TIME	VENDOR	PURPOSE

Weekly Wedding Planning

WEEK OF: ....

MONDAY

TUESDAY

WEDNESDAY

THURSDAY

FRIDAY

SATURDAY

WEDDING TO DO LIST

- [ ]
- [ ]
- [ ]
- [ ]
- [ ]
- [ ]
- [ ]
- [ ]
- [ ]
- [ ]
- [ ]
- [ ]
- [ ]
- [ ]
- [ ]
- [ ]

APPOINTMENTS & MEETINGS

DATE	TIME	VENDOR	PURPOSE

Weekly Wedding Planning

WEEK OF: _____

MONDAY

WEDNESDAY, TUESDAY...

WEDDING TO DO LIST

☐ _____
☐ _____
☐ _____
☐ _____
☐ _____
☐ _____
☐ _____
☐ _____
☐ _____
☐ _____
☐ _____
☐ _____
☐ _____
☐ _____
☐ _____
☐ _____

APPOINTMENTS & MEETINGS			
DATE	TIME	VENDOR	PURPOSE

MONDAY

TUESDAY

WEDNESDAY

THURSDAY

FRIDAY

SATURDAY

Weekly Wedding Planning

WEEK OF: ....

MONDAY

TUESDAY

WEDNESDAY

THURSDAY

FRIDAY

SATURDAY

WEDDING TO DO LIST

- [ ] ....
- [ ] ....
- [ ] ....
- [ ] ....
- [ ] ....
- [ ] ....
- [ ] ....
- [ ] ....
- [ ] ....
- [ ] ....
- [ ] ....
- [ ] ....
- [ ] ....
- [ ] ....
- [ ] ....
- [ ] ....

APPOINTMENTS & MEETINGS

DATE	TIME	VENDOR	PURPOSE

Weekly Wedding Planning

WEEK OF: _____

MONDAY

TUESDAY

WEDNESDAY

THURSDAY

FRIDAY

SATURDAY

WEDDING TO DO LIST

- ☐ _____
- ☐ _____
- ☐ _____
- ☐ _____
- ☐ _____
- ☐ _____
- ☐ _____
- ☐ _____
- ☐ _____
- ☐ _____
- ☐ _____
- ☐ _____
- ☐ _____
- ☐ _____
- ☐ _____

APPOINTMENTS & MEETINGS

DATE	TIME	VENDOR	PURPOSE

Weekly Wedding Planning

WEEK OF: ....

MONDAY

TUESDAY

WEDNESDAY

THURSDAY

FRIDAY

SATURDAY

WEDDING TO DO LIST

- ☐ ....
- ☐ ....
- ☐ ....
- ☐ ....
- ☐ ....
- ☐ ....
- ☐ ....
- ☐ ....
- ☐ ....
- ☐ ....
- ☐ ....
- ☐ ....
- ☐ ....
- ☐ ....
- ☐ ....

APPOINTMENTS & MEETINGS

DATE	TIME	VENDOR	PURPOSE

Weekly Wedding Planning

WEEK OF: ....

MONDAY

TUESDAY

WEDNESDAY

THURSDAY

FRIDAY

SATURDAY

WEDDING TO DO LIST

- [ ] _____
- [ ] _____
- [ ] _____
- [ ] _____
- [ ] _____
- [ ] _____
- [ ] _____
- [ ] _____
- [ ] _____
- [ ] _____
- [ ] _____
- [ ] _____
- [ ] _____
- [ ] _____
- [ ] _____

APPOINTMENTS & MEETINGS

DATE	TIME	VENDOR	PURPOSE

Weekly Wedding Planning

WEEK OF: ....

MONDAY

TUESDAY

WEDNESDAY

THURSDAY

FRIDAY

SATURDAY

WEDDING TO DO LIST

- ☐ _____
- ☐ _____
- ☐ _____
- ☐ _____
- ☐ _____
- ☐ _____
- ☐ _____
- ☐ _____
- ☐ _____
- ☐ _____
- ☐ _____
- ☐ _____
- ☐ _____
- ☐ _____
- ☐ _____

APPOINTMENTS & MEETINGS			
DATE	TIME	VENDOR	PURPOSE

Weekly Wedding Planning

WEEK OF: _____

MONDAY

TUESDAY

WEDNESDAY

THURSDAY

FRIDAY

SATURDAY

WEDDING TO DO LIST

- ☐ _____
- ☐ _____
- ☐ _____
- ☐ _____
- ☐ _____
- ☐ _____
- ☐ _____
- ☐ _____
- ☐ _____
- ☐ _____
- ☐ _____
- ☐ _____
- ☐ _____
- ☐ _____
- ☐ _____

APPOINTMENTS & MEETINGS			
DATE	TIME	VENDOR	PURPOSE

Wedding Planner

- PLANNING GUIDELINE -

- SET THE DATE
- SET YOUR BUDGET
- CONSIDER WEDDING THEMES
- PLAN ENGAGEMENT PARTY
- RESEARCH POSSIBLE VENUES
- START RESEARCHING TUXEDOS
- RESEARCH PHOTOGRAPHERS
- RESEARCH VIDEOGRAPHERS
- RESEARCH DJS/ENTERTAINMENT

- CONSIDER FLORISTS
- RESEARCH CATERERS
- DECIDE ON OFFICIANT
- CREATE INITIAL GUEST LIST
- CHOOSE WEDDING PARTY
- CONSIDER ACCESSORIES
- REGISTER WITH GIFT REGISTRY
- DISCUSS HONEYMOON IDEAS
- RESEARCH WEDDING RINGS

- CONSIDER MUSIC CHOICES
- CONSIDER MUSIC LIST
- CONSIDER TRANSPORTATION
- CREATE INITIAL GUEST LIST
- CHOOSE WEDDING PARTY
- BRIDESMAN SUIT
- BOOK TENTATIVE HOTELS
- CONSIDER BEAUTY SALONS
- CONSIDER SHOES & OTHER

Things To Do	Status

TOP PRIORITIES

NOTES & IDEAS

APPOINTMENTS & REMINDERS

Wedding Planner

- PLANNING GUIDELINE -

9 *Months* BEFORE WEDDING

- [ ] FINALIZE GUEST LIST
- [ ] ORDER INVITATIONS
- [ ] PLAN YOUR RECEPTION
- [ ] BOOK PHOTOGRAPHER
- [ ] BOOK VIDEOGRAPHER
- [ ] CHOOSE WEDDING TUXEDO

- [ ] ORDER BRIDESMAN SUIT
- [ ] RESERVE WEDDING TUXEDO
- [ ] ARRANGE TRANSPORTATION
- [ ] BOOK WEDDING VENUE
- [ ] BOOK RECEPTION VENUE
- [ ] PLAN HONEYMOON

- [ ] BOOK FLORIST
- [ ] BOOK DJ/ENTERTAINMENT
- [ ] BOOK CATERER
- [ ] CHOOSE WEDDING CAKE
- [ ] BOOK OFFICIANT
- [ ] BOOK ROOMS FOR GUESTS

Things To Do	Status

TOP PRIORITIES

NOTES & IDEAS

APPOINTMENTS & REMINDERS

Wedding Planner

- PLANNING GUIDELINE -

6 Months BEFORE WEDDING

☐ ORDER THANK YOU NOTES

☐ REVIEW RECEPTION DETAILS

☐ MAKE APPT FOR FITTING

☐ CONFIRM TUXEDOS

☐ OBTAIN MARRIAGE LICENSE

☐ BOOK HAIR STYLIST

☐ CONFIRM MUSIC SELECTION

☐ WRITE VOWS

☐ BOOK REHEARSAL DINNER

☐ PLAN REHEARSAL

☐ CONFIRM HOTEL ROOMS

☐ SHOP FOR WEDDING RINGS

☐ PLAN DECORATIONS

☐ CHOOSE BOUTONNIERES TYPE

☐ FINALIZE GUEST LIST

☐ UPDATE PASSPORTS

Things To Do	Status

TOP PRIORITIES

NOTES & IDEAS

APPOINTMENTS & REMINDERS

Wedding Planner

- PLANNING GUIDELINE -

4 Months BEFORE WEDDING

- ☐ MAIL OUT INVITATIONS
- ☐ MEET WITH OFFICIANT
- ☐ BUY WEDDING FAVORS
- ☐ BUY WEDDING PARTY GIFTS
- ☐ PURCHASE SHOES
- ☐ FINALIZE THANK YOU CARDS

- ☐ FINALIZE HONEYMOON PLANS
- ☐ ATTEND FIRST TUXEDO FITTING
- ☐ FINALIZE VOWS
- ☐ FINALIZE RECEPTION MENU
- ☐ KEEP TRACK OF RSVPS
- ☐ BOOK PHOTO SESSION

- ☐ CONFIRM CATERER
- ☐ FINALIZE RING FITTING
- ☐ CONFIRM FLOWERS
- ☐ CONFIRM BAND
- ☐ SHOP FOR HONEYMOON

Things To Do   Status

TOP PRIORITIES

NOTES & IDEAS

APPOINTMENTS & REMINDERS

Wedding Planner

- PLANNING GUIDELINE -

- ☐ CHOOSE YOUR MC
- ☐ REQUEST SPECIAL TOASTS
- ☐ ARRANGE TRANSPORTATION
- ☐ CHOOSE YOUR HAIR STYLE
- ☐ ARRANGE LEGAL DOCS
- ☐ CREATE WEDDING SCHEDULE

- ☐ CONFIRM CAKE CHOICES
- ☐ CONFIRM MENU (FINAL)
- ☐ CONFIRM SEATING
- ☐ CONFIRM VIDEOGRAPHER
- ☐ FINALIZE WEDDING DUTIES

- ☐ CONFIRM BRIDESMAN SUIT
- ☐ MEET WITH DJ/MC
- ☐ FINAL TUXEDO FITTING
- ☐ WRAP WEDDIING PARTY GIFTS
- ☐ CONFIRM FINAL GUEST COUNT

Things To Do	Status

TOP PRIORITIES

NOTES & IDEAS

APPOINTMENTS & REMINDERS

- [ ] PAYMENT TO VENDORS
- [ ] PACK FOR HONEYMOON
- [ ] CONFIRM HOTEL RESERVATION
- [ ] GIVE SCHEDULE TO PARTY
- [ ] DELIVER LICENSE TO OFFICIANT
- [ ] CONFIRM WITH VENDORS

- [ ] PICK UP TUXEDO
- [ ] GIVE MUSIC LIST TO DJ/BAND
- [ ] CONFIRM SHOES FIT
- [ ] CONFIRM TRANSPORTATION
- [ ] MONEY FOR GRATUITIES

- [ ] CONFIRM RINGS FIT
- [ ] CONFIRM TRAVEL PLANS
- [ ] CONFIRM HOTELS FOR GUESTS
- [ ] OTHER: _____
- [ ] OTHER: _____

Things To Do   Status

TOP PRIORITIES

NOTES & IDEAS

APPOINTMENTS & REMINDERS

Wedding Planner

- PLANNING GUIDELINE -

- ☐ ATTEND REHEARSAL DINNER
- ☐ FINISH HONEYMOON PACKING
- ☐ GREET OUT OF TOWN GUESTS

- ☐ CHECK WEATHER TO PREPARE
- ☐ CHECK ON WEDDING VENUE

- ☐ GIVE GIFTS TO WEDDING PARTY
- ☐ CONFIRM RINGS FIT
- ☐ GET A GOOD NIGHT'S SLEEP

Things To Do	Status

TOP PRIORITIES

NOTES & IDEAS

APPOINTMENTS & REMINDERS

Your Special Day!

Day of WEDDING

- ☐ GET YOUR HAIR DONE
- ☐ HAVE A LIGHT BREAKFAST

- ☐ GIVE RINGS TO BEST WOMAN
- ☐ ENJOY YOUR SPECIAL DAY!

MR ♥ MRS

Wedding Attire Planner

WEDDING ATTIRE EXPENSE TRACKER

ITEM/PURCHASE	STATUS ✓	DATE PAID	TOTAL COST

NOTES & REMINDERS

TOTAL COST:

Notes:

WEDDING ATTIRE DETAILS

Venue Planner

VENUE EXPENSE TRACKER

ITEM/PURCHASE	STATUS ✓	DATE PAID	TOTAL COST

NOTES & REMINDERS

TOTAL COST:

Notes:

- Mr & Mrs -

VENUE PLANNING DETAILS

Catering Planner

CATERING EXPENSE TRACKER

ITEM/PURCHASE	STATUS ✓	DATE PAID	TOTAL COST

NOTES & REMINDERS	
	TOTAL COST:

Notes:

CATERING PLANNER DETAILS

Entertainment Planner

ENTERTAINMENT EXPENSE TRACKER

ITEM/PURCHASE	STATUS ✓	DATE PAID	TOTAL COST

NOTES & REMINDERS

TOTAL COST:

Notes:

Love

ENTERTAINMENT DETAILS

Videographer Planner

VIDEOGRAPHER EXPENSE TRACKER			
ITEM/PURCHASE	STATUS ✓	DATE PAID	TOTAL COST

NOTES & REMINDERS

TOTAL COST:

Notes:

VIDEOGRAPHER DETAILS

Photographer Planner

PHOTOGRAPHER EXPENSE TRACKER

ITEM/PURCHASE	STATUS ✓	DATE PAID	TOTAL COST

NOTES & REMINDERS	
	TOTAL COST:

Notes:

PHOTOGRAPHER DETAILS

Florist Planner

FLORIST EXPENSE TRACKER			
ITEM/PURCHASE	STATUS ✓	DATE PAID	TOTAL COST
☐			
☐			
☐			
☐			
☐			

NOTES & REMINDERS

TOTAL COST:

Notes:

FLORIST PLANNING DETAILS

Extra Wedding Costs

MISC WEDDING EXPENSE TRACKER

ITEM/PURCHASE	STATUS ✓	DATE PAID	TOTAL COST

NOTES & REMINDERS

TOTAL COST:

Notes:

MISC WEDDING DETAILS

Bachelor Party Planner

EVENT DETAILS

DATE

TIME

VENUE

THEME

HOST

OTHER

GUEST LIST

FIRST NAME	LAST NAME	R

TIME	SCHEDULE OF EVENTS

SUPPLIES & SHOPPING LIST

- ☐
- ☐
- ☐
- ☐
- ☐
- ☐
- ☐
- ☐
- ☐
- ☐
- ☐
- ☐
- ☐
- ☐
- ☐
- ☐

NOTES & REMINDERS

love

Reception Planner

HORS D'OEUVRES

1st COURSE:

3rd COURSE:

2nd COURSE:

4th COURSE:

MEAL PLANNING NOTES

Wedding Planning Notes

_____

_____

_____

_____

_____

_____

_____

_____

_____

_____

_____

_____

_____

_____

_____

_____

_____

_____

_____

_____

_____

_____

_____

_____

Wedding to do List

PLANNING FOR THE BIG DAY

Wedding Guest List

NAME	ADDRESS	PHONE #	# IN PARTY	RSVP: ✓

Wedding Guest List

NAME	ADDRESS	PHONE #	# IN PARTY	RSVP: ✓

Wedding Guest List

NAME	ADDRESS	PHONE #	# IN PARTY	RSVP: ✓

Wedding Guest List

NAME	ADDRESS	PHONE #	# IN PARTY	RSVP: ✓

Wedding Guest List

NAME	ADDRESS	PHONE #	# IN PARTY	RSVP: ✓

Wedding Guest List

NAME	ADDRESS	PHONE #	# IN PARTY	RSVP: ✓

Wedding Guest List

NAME	ADDRESS	PHONE #	# IN PARTY	RSVP: ✓

Wedding Guest List

NAME	ADDRESS	PHONE #	# IN PARTY	RSVP: ✓

Wedding Guest List

NAME	ADDRESS	PHONE #	# IN PARTY	RSVP: ✓

Wedding Guest List

NAME	ADDRESS	PHONE #	# IN PARTY	RSVP: ✓

Wedding Guest List

NAME	ADDRESS	PHONE #	# IN PARTY	RSVP: ✓

Wedding Guest List

NAME	ADDRESS	PHONE #	# IN PARTY	RSVP: ✓

Wedding Seating Chart

Table #

Table #

Love

TABLE #:

1:

2:

3:

4:

5:

6:

7:

8:

TABLE #:

1:

2:

3:

4:

5:

6:

7:

8:

Wedding Seating Chart

Table #

Table #

love

TABLE #:

1 :

2 :

3 :

4 :

5 :

6 :

7 :

8 :

TABLE #:

1 :

2 :

3 :

4 :

5 :

6 :

7 :

8 :

Wedding Seating Chart

Table #

Table #

TABLE #:
1 :
2 :
3 :
4 :
5 :
6 :
7 :
8 :

TABLE #:
1 :
2 :
3 :
4 :
5 :
6 :
7 :
8 :

Wedding Seating Chart

Table #

TABLE #:

1:

2:

3:

4:

5:

6:

7:

8:

Table #

TABLE #:

1:

2:

3:

4:

5:

6:

7:

8:

Wedding Seating Chart

Table #

Table #

Wedding Seating Chart

Table #

Table #

TABLE #:

1:

2:

3:

4:

5:

6:

7:

8:

TABLE #:

1:

2:

3:

4:

5:

6:

7:

8:

Wedding Seating Chart

Table #

Table #

TABLE #:

1:

2:

3:

4:

5:

6:

7:

8:

TABLE #:

1:

2:

3:

4:

5:

6:

7:

8:

Wedding Seating Chart

Table #

Table #

TABLE #:	
1:	
2:	
3:	
4:	
5:	
6:	
7:	
8:	

TABLE #:	
1:	
2:	
3:	
4:	
5:	
6:	
7:	
8:	

Wedding Seating Chart

Table #

Table #

TABLE #:
1 :
2 :
3 :
4 :
5 :
6 :
7 :
8 :

TABLE #:
1 :
2 :
3 :
4 :
5 :
6 :
7 :
8 :

Wedding Seating Chart

Table #

Table #

TABLE #:	
1:	
2:	
3:	
4:	
5:	
6:	
7:	
8:	

TABLE #:	
1:	
2:	
3:	
4:	
5:	
6:	
7:	
8:	

Wedding Seating Chart

Table #

Table #

TABLE #:

1:

2:

3:

4:

5:

6:

7:

8:

TABLE #:

1:

2:

3:

4:

5:

6:

7:

8:

Wedding Seating Chart

Table #

Table #

TABLE #:

1:

2:

3:

4:

5:

6:

7:

8:

TABLE #:

1:

2:

3:

4:

5:

6:

7:

8:

Wedding Seating Chart

Table #

Table #

TABLE #:

1:

2:

3:

4:

5:

6:

7:

8:

TABLE #:

1:

2:

3:

4:

5:

6:

7:

8:

Wedding Seating Chart

Table #

Table #

TABLE #:	
1 :	
2 :	
3 :	
4 :	
5 :	
6 :	
7 :	
8 :	

TABLE #:	
1 :	
2 :	
3 :	
4 :	
5 :	
6 :	
7 :	
8 :	

Wedding Seating Chart

Table #

Table #

TABLE #:

1:

2:

3:

4:

5:

6:

7:

8:

TABLE #:

1:

2:

3:

4:

5:

6:

7:

8:

Wedding Seating Chart

Table #

TABLE #:

1 :

2 :

3 :

4 :

5 :

6 :

7 :

8 :

Table #

TABLE #:

1 :

2 :

3 :

4 :

5 :

6 :

7 :

8 :

Wedding Seating Chart

Table #

Table #

TABLE #:

1:

2:

3:

4:

5:

6:

7:

8:

TABLE #:

1:

2:

3:

4:

5:

6:

7:

8:

Wedding Seating Chart

Table #

Table #

TABLE #:
1 :
2 :
3 :
4 :
5 :
6 :
7 :
8 :

TABLE #:
1 :
2 :
3 :
4 :
5 :
6 :
7 :
8 :

Wedding Seating Chart

Table #

TABLE #:

1:

2:

3:

4:

5:

6:

7:

8:

Table #

TABLE #:

1:

2:

3:

4:

5:

6:

7:

8:

Wedding Seating Chart

Table #

Table #

TABLE #:

1:

2:

3:

4:

5:

6:

7:

8:

TABLE #:

1:

2:

3:

4:

5:

6:

7:

8:

Wedding Seating Chart

Table #

Table #

TABLE #:

1:

2:

3:

4:

5:

6:

7:

8:

TABLE #:

1:

2:

3:

4:

5:

6:

7:

8:

Wedding Seating Chart

Table #

Table #

TABLE #:

1:

2:

3:

4:

5:

6:

7:

8:

TABLE #:

1:

2:

3:

4:

5:

6:

7:

8:

Wedding Seating Chart

Table #

Table #

TABLE #:

1:

2:

3:

4:

5:

6:

7:

8:

TABLE #:

1:

2:

3:

4:

5:

6:

7:

8:

Wedding Seating Chart

Table #

Table #

TABLE #:

1 :

2 :

3 :

4 :

5 :

6 :

7 :

8 :

TABLE #:

1 :

2 :

3 :

4 :

5 :

6 :

7 :

8 :

Wedding Seating Chart

Table #

Table #

Wedding Seating Chart

Table #

Table #

TABLE #:
1 :
2 :
3 :
4 :
5 :
6 :
7 :
8 :

TABLE #:
1 :
2 :
3 :
4 :
5 :
6 :
7 :
8 :

Wedding Seating Chart

Table

TABLE #:

1:	2:	3:	4:	5:	6:	7:	8:
9:	10:	11:	12:	13:	14:	15:	16:

Table

TABLE #:

1:	2:	3:	4:	5:	6:	7:	8:
9:	10:	11:	12:	13:	14:	15:	16:

Wedding Seating Chart

Table

TABLE #:

1:	2:	3:	4:	5:	6:	7:	8:
9:	10:	11:	12:	13:	14:	15:	16:

Table

TABLE #:

1:	2:	3:	4:	5:	6:	7:	8:
9:	10:	11:	12:	13:	14:	15:	16:

Wedding Seating Chart

Table

TABLE #:

1:	2:	3:	4:	5:	6:	7:	8:
9:	10:	11:	12:	13:	14:	15:	16:

Table

TABLE #:

1:	2:	3:	4:	5:	6:	7:	8:
9:	10:	11:	12:	13:	14:	15:	16:

Wedding Seating Chart

Table #

TABLE #:

1:	2:	3:	4:	5:	6:	7:	8:
9:	10:	11:	12:	13:	14:	15:	16:

Table #

TABLE #:

1:	2:	3:	4:	5:	6:	7:	8:
9:	10:	11:	12:	13:	14:	15:	16:

Wedding Seating Chart

Table

TABLE #:

1:	2:	3:	4:	5:	6:	7:	8:
9:	10:	11:	12:	13:	14:	15:	16:

Table

TABLE #:

1:	2:	3:	4:	5:	6:	7:	8:
9:	10:	11:	12:	13:	14:	15:	16:

Wedding Seating Chart

Table

TABLE #:

1:	2:	3:	4:	5:	6:	7:	8:
9:	10:	11:	12:	13:	14:	15:	16:

Table

TABLE #:

1:	2:	3:	4:	5:	6:	7:	8:
9:	10:	11:	12:	13:	14:	15:	16:

Wedding Seating Chart

Table

TABLE #:

1:	2:	3:	4:	5:	6:	7:	8:
9:	10:	11:	12:	13:	14:	15:	16:

Table

TABLE #:

1:	2:	3:	4:	5:	6:	7:	8:
9:	10:	11:	12:	13:	14:	15:	16:

Wedding Seating Chart

Table #

TABLE #:

1:	2:	3:	4:	5:	6:	7:	8:
9:	10:	11:	12:	13:	14:	15:	16:

Table #

TABLE #:

1:	2:	3:	4:	5:	6:	7:	8:
9:	10:	11:	12:	13:	14:	15:	16:

Wedding Seating Chart

Table #

TABLE #:

1:	2:	3:	4:	5:	6:	7:	8:
9:	10:	11:	12:	13:	14:	15:	16:

Table #

TABLE #:

1:	2:	3:	4:	5:	6:	7:	8:
9:	10:	11:	12:	13:	14:	15:	16:

Wedding Seating Chart

Table

TABLE #:

1:	2:	3:	4:	5:	6:	7:	8:
9:	10:	11:	12:	13:	14:	15:	16:

Table

TABLE #:

1:	2:	3:	4:	5:	6:	7:	8:
9:	10:	11:	12:	13:	14:	15:	16:

Wedding Seating Chart

Table #

TABLE #:

1:	2:	3:	4:	5:	6:	7:	8:
9:	10:	11:	12:	13:	14:	15:	16:

Table #

TABLE #:

1:	2:	3:	4:	5:	6:	7:	8:
9:	10:	11:	12:	13:	14:	15:	16:

Made in the USA
Columbia, SC
06 December 2021